This
Mindfulness Daily Journal
Belongs To

_____

_____

_____

Morning Routine

Date: _____

Today's positive Affirmation

Today's personal Goal

(Write down what you want to achieve for yourself today)

_____

_____

Today's Intention

(Write down how you want this day to be)

5 Things I am grateful for

1 _____
2 _____
3 _____
4 _____
5 _____

Mindfulness Exercise

(Notice five things that you can see and write them down).

# 1	
# 2	
# 3	
# 4	
# 5	

Evening Routine

This went well today

5 Things I am proud of

1

2

3

4

5

This made me feel happy

My Thoughts about today

Morning Routine

Date: _____

Today's positive Affirmation

```
[                                                            ]
```

Today's personal Goal

(Write down what you want to achieve for yourself today)

_____

_____

Today's Intention

(Write down how you want this day to be)

```
[                                                            ]
```

5 Things I am grateful for

1 _____
2 _____
3 _____
4 _____
5 _____

Mindfulness Exercise

(Notice five things that you can see and write them down).

# 1	
# 2	
# 3	
# 4	
# 5	

Evening Routine

This went well today

5 Things I am proud of

#1

#2

#3

#4

#5

This made me feel happy

My Thoughts about today

Morning Routine

Date: _____

Today's positive Affirmation

Today's personal Goal

(Write down what you want to achieve for yourself today)

_____

_____

Today's Intention

(Write down how you want this day to be)

5 Things I am grateful for

# 1	
# 2	
# 3	
# 4	
# 5	

Mindfulness Exercise

(Notice five things that you can see and write them down).

# 1	
# 2	
# 3	
# 4	
# 5	

Evening Routine

This went well today

5 Things I am proud of

1

2

3

4

5

This made me feel happy

My Thoughts about today

Morning Routine

Date: _____

Today's positive Affirmation

```


```

Today's personal Goal
(Write down what you want to achieve for yourself today)

_____

_____

Today's Intention
(Write down how you want this day to be)

```


```

5 Things I am grateful for

#1 _____
#2 _____
#3 _____
#4 _____
#5 _____

Mindfulness Exercise
(Notice five things that you can see and write them down).

| #1 |
| #2 |
| #3 |
| #4 |
| #5 |

Evening Routine

This went well today

5 Things I am proud of

1

2

3

4

5

This made me feel happy

My Thoughts about today

Morning Routine

Date: _____

Today's positive Affirmation

Today's personal Goal

(Write down what you want to achieve for yourself today)

_____

_____

Today's Intention

(Write down how you want this day to be)

5 Things I am grateful for

1 _____
2 _____
3 _____
4 _____
5 _____

Mindfulness Exercise

(Notice five things that you can see and write them down).

1
2
3
4
5

Evening Routine

This went well today

5 Things I am proud of

#1 _____
#2 _____
#3 _____
#4 _____
#5 _____

This made me feel happy

My Thoughts about today

_____
_____
_____
_____
_____
_____
_____
_____
_____

Morning Routine

Date: _____

Today's positive Affirmation

Today's personal Goal

(Write down what you want to achieve for yourself today)

_____

_____

Today's Intention

(Write down how you want this day to be)

5 Things I am grateful for

1 _____
2 _____
3 _____
4 _____
5 _____

Mindfulness Exercise

(Notice five things that you can see and write them down).

# 1	
# 2	
# 3	
# 4	
# 5	

Evening Routine

This went well today

5 Things I am proud of

#1 _____

#2 _____

#3 _____

#4 _____

#5 _____

This made me feel happy

My Thoughts about today

_____

_____

_____

_____

_____

_____

_____

_____

_____

_____

Morning Routine

Date: _____

Today's positive Affirmation

[ ]

Today's personal Goal

(Write down what you want to achieve for yourself today)

_____

_____

Today's Intention

(Write down how you want this day to be)

[ ]

5 Things I am grateful for

1 _____
2 _____
3 _____
4 _____
5 _____

Mindfulness Exercise

(Notice five things that you can see and write them down).

# 1	
# 2	
# 3	
# 4	
# 5	

Evening Routine

This went well today

5 Things I am proud of

1
2
3
4
5

This made me feel happy

My Thoughts about today

Morning Routine

Date: _____

Today's positive Affirmation

Today's personal Goal
(Write down what you want to achieve for yourself today)

Today's Intention
(Write down how you want this day to be)

5 Things I am grateful for

1
2
3
4
5

Mindfulness Exercise
(Notice five things that you can see and write them down).

1
2
3
4
5

Evening Routine

This went well today

5 Things I am proud of

1
2
3
4
5

This made me feel happy

My Thoughts about today

Morning Routine

Date: _____

Today's positive Affirmation

Today's personal Goal

(Write down what you want to achieve for yourself today)

_____

_____

Today's Intention

(Write down how you want this day to be)

5 Things I am grateful for

#1 _____
#2 _____
#3 _____
#4 _____
#5 _____

Mindfulness Exercise

(Notice five things that you can see and write them down).

#1
#2
#3
#4
#5

Evening Routine

This went well today

5 Things I am proud of

1

2

3

4

5

This made me feel happy

My Thoughts about today

Morning Routine

Date: _____

Today's positive Affirmation

| |
| |

Today's personal Goal

(Write down what you want to achieve for yourself today)

_____

_____

Today's Intention

(Write down how you want this day to be)

| |
| |

5 Things I am grateful for

1 _____
2 _____
3 _____
4 _____
5 _____

Mindfulness Exercise

(Notice five things that you can see and write them down).

# 1	
# 2	
# 3	
# 4	
# 5	

Evening Routine

This went well today

5 Things I am proud of

1 _____
2 _____
3 _____
4 _____
5 _____

This made me feel happy

My Thoughts about today

_____
_____
_____
_____
_____
_____
_____
_____
_____

Morning Routine

Date: _____

Today's positive Affirmation

Today's personal Goal

(Write down what you want to achieve for yourself today)

Today's Intention

(Write down how you want this day to be)

---

5 Things I am grateful for

1 _____
2 _____
3 _____
4 _____
5 _____

Mindfulness Exercise

(Notice five things that you can see and write them down).

# 1	
# 2	
# 3	
# 4	
# 5	

Evening Routine

This went well today

5 Things I am proud of

\# 1 _____

\# 2 _____

\# 3 _____

\# 4 _____

\# 5 _____

This made me feel happy

My Thoughts about today

_____

_____

_____

_____

_____

_____

_____

_____

_____

_____

Morning Routine

Date: _____

Today's positive Affirmation

Today's personal Goal
(Write down what you want to achieve for yourself today)

Today's Intention
(Write down how you want this day to be)

5 Things I am grateful for

#1
#2
#3
#4
#5

Mindfulness Exercise
(Notice five things that you can see and write them down).

#1
#2
#3
#4
#5

Evening Routine

This went well today

5 Things I am proud of

#1

#2

#3

#4

#5

This made me feel happy

My Thoughts about today

Morning Routine

Date: _____

Today's positive Affirmation

```



```

Today's personal Goal
(Write down what you want to achieve for yourself today)

_____

_____

Today's Intention
(Write down how you want this day to be)

```



```

5 Things I am grateful for

#1 _____
#2 _____
#3 _____
#4 _____
#5 _____

Mindfulness Exercise
(Notice five things that you can see and write them down).

#1	
#2	
#3	
#4	
#5	

Evening Routine

This went well today

5 Things I am proud of

1 _____
2 _____
3 _____
4 _____
5 _____

This made me feel happy

My Thoughts about today

_____
_____
_____
_____
_____
_____
_____
_____
_____

Morning Routine

Date: _____

Today's positive Affirmation

```
[                                                    ]
```

Today's personal Goal
(Write down what you want to achieve for yourself today)

_____

_____

Today's Intention
(Write down how you want this day to be)

```
[                                                    ]
```

5 Things I am grateful for

1 _____
2 _____
3 _____
4 _____
5 _____

Mindfulness Exercise
(Notice five things that you can see and write them down).

# 1	
# 2	
# 3	
# 4	
# 5	

Evening Routine

This went well today

5 Things I am proud of

#1

#2

#3

#4

#5

This made me feel happy

My Thoughts about today

Morning Routine

Date: _____

Today's positive Affirmation

```
[                                                                    ]
```

Today's personal Goal   (Write down what you want to achieve for yourself today)

_____

_____

Today's Intention   (Write down how you want this day to be)

```
[                                                                    ]
```

5 Things I am grateful for

#1 _____
#2 _____
#3 _____
#4 _____
#5 _____

Mindfulness Exercise   (Notice five things that you can see and write them down).

#1	
#2	
#3	
#4	
#5	

Evening Routine

This went well today

5 Things I am proud of

#1 _____

#2 _____

#3 _____

#4 _____

#5 _____

This made me feel happy

My Thoughts about today

_____
_____
_____
_____
_____
_____
_____
_____
_____
_____

Morning Routine

Date: _____

Today's positive Affirmation

_____

Today's personal Goal

(Write down what you want to achieve for yourself today)

_____

_____

Today's Intention

(Write down how you want this day to be)

_____

5 Things I am grateful for

#1 _____
#2 _____
#3 _____
#4 _____
#5 _____

Mindfulness Exercise

(Notice five things that you can see and write them down).

#1 _____
#2 _____
#3 _____
#4 _____
#5 _____

Evening Routine

This went well today

5 Things I am proud of

#1

#2

#3

#4

#5

This made me feel happy

My Thoughts about today

Morning Routine

Date: _____

Today's positive Affirmation

> (empty box)

Today's personal Goal

(Write down what you want to achieve for yourself today)

_____

_____

Today's Intention

(Write down how you want this day to be)

> (empty box)

5 Things I am grateful for

#1 _____
#2 _____
#3 _____
#4 _____
#5 _____

Mindfulness Exercise

(Notice five things that you can see and write them down).

#1	
#2	
#3	
#4	
#5	

Evening Routine

This went well today

5 Things I am proud of

#1

#2

#3

#4

#5

This made me feel happy

My Thoughts about today

Morning Routine

Date: _____

Today's positive Affirmation

┌───┐
│   │
│   │
│   │
└───┘

Today's personal Goal

(Write down what you want to achieve for yourself today)

_____

_____

Today's Intention

(Write down how you want this day to be)

┌───┐
│   │
│   │
│   │
└───┘

5 Things I am grateful for

1 _____

2 _____

3 _____

4 _____

5 _____

Mindfulness Exercise

(Notice five things that you can see and write them down).

# 1	
# 2	
# 3	
# 4	
# 5	

Evening Routine

This went well today

5 Things I am proud of

#1 _____

#2 _____

#3 _____

#4 _____

#5 _____

This made me feel happy

My Thoughts about today

_____

_____

_____

_____

_____

_____

_____

_____

_____

Morning Routine

Date: _____

Today's positive Affirmation

+---+
| |
| |
| |
| |
+---+

Today's personal Goal

(Write down what you want to achieve for yourself today)

_____

_____

Today's Intention

(Write down how you want this day to be)

+---+
| |
| |
| |
| |
+---+

5 Things I am grateful for

1 _____
2 _____
3 _____
4 _____
5 _____

Mindfulness Exercise

(Notice five things that you can see and write them down).

# 1	
# 2	
# 3	
# 4	
# 5	

Evening Routine

This went well today

5 Things I am proud of

#1

#2

#3

#4

#5

This made me feel happy

My Thoughts about today

Morning Routine

Date: _____

Today's positive Affirmation

```
[                                              ]
```

Today's personal Goal

(Write down what you want to achieve for yourself today)

_____

_____

Today's Intention

(Write down how you want this day to be)

```
[                                              ]
```

5 Things I am grateful for

#1 _____
#2 _____
#3 _____
#4 _____
#5 _____

Mindfulness Exercise

(Notice five things that you can see and write them down).

#1 _____
#2 _____
#3 _____
#4 _____
#5 _____

Evening Routine

This went well today

5 Things I am proud of

1 _____

2 _____

3 _____

4 _____

5 _____

This made me feel happy

My Thoughts about today

Morning Routine

Date: _____

Today's positive Affirmation

_____

Today's personal Goal

(Write down what you want to achieve for yourself today)

_____

Today's Intention

(Write down how you want this day to be)

_____

5 Things I am grateful for

1 _____
2 _____
3 _____
4 _____
5 _____

Mindfulness Exercise

(Notice five things that you can see and write them down).

1 _____
2 _____
3 _____
4 _____
5 _____

Evening Routine

This went well today

5 Things I am proud of

#1 _____

#2 _____

#3 _____

#4 _____

#5 _____

This made me feel happy

My Thoughts about today

_____

_____

_____

_____

_____

_____

_____

_____

_____

Morning Routine

Date: _____

Today's positive Affirmation

┌───┐
│   │
│   │
│   │
└───┘

Today's personal Goal

(Write down what you want to achieve for yourself today)

_____

_____

Today's Intention

(Write down how you want this day to be)

┌───┐
│   │
│   │
│   │
└───┘

5 Things I am grateful for

1 _____

2 _____

3 _____

4 _____

5 _____

Mindfulness Exercise

(Notice five things that you can see and write them down).

| # 1 |
| # 2 |
| # 3 |
| # 4 |
| # 5 |

Evening Routine

This went well today

5 Things I am proud of

#1 _____

#2 _____

#3 _____

#4 _____

#5 _____

This made me feel happy

My Thoughts about today

_____

_____

_____

_____

_____

_____

_____

_____

_____

Morning Routine

Date: _____

Today's positive Affirmation

```
┌────────────────────────────────────┐
│                                    │
│                                    │
│                                    │
│                                    │
└────────────────────────────────────┘
```

Today's personal Goal

(Write down what you want to achieve for yourself today)

_____

_____

Today's Intention

(Write down how you want this day to be)

```
┌────────────────────────────────────┐
│                                    │
│                                    │
│                                    │
│                                    │
└────────────────────────────────────┘
```

5 Things I am grateful for

1 _____
2 _____
3 _____
4 _____
5 _____

Mindfulness Exercise

(Notice five things that you can see and write them down).

# 1	
# 2	
# 3	
# 4	
# 5	

Evening Routine

This went well today

5 Things I am proud of

1

2

3

4

5

This made me feel happy

My Thoughts about today

Morning Routine

Date: _____

Today's positive Affirmation

> [blank box]

Today's personal Goal

(Write down what you want to achieve for yourself today)

_____

_____

Today's Intention

(Write down how you want this day to be)

> [blank box]

5 Things I am grateful for

#1 _____

#2 _____

#3 _____

#4 _____

#5 _____

Mindfulness Exercise

(Notice five things that you can see and write them down).

#1	
#2	
#3	
#4	
#5	

Evening Routine

This went well today

5 Things I am proud of

\# 1

\# 2

\# 3

\# 4

\# 5

This made me feel happy

My Thoughts about today

Morning Routine

Date: _____

Today's positive Affirmation

```
┌────────────────────────────────────────────────────┐
│                                                    │
│                                                    │
│                                                    │
│                                                    │
└────────────────────────────────────────────────────┘
```

Today's personal Goal

(Write down what you want to achieve for yourself today)

_____

_____

Today's Intention

(Write down how you want this day to be)

```
┌────────────────────────────────────────────────────┐
│                                                    │
│                                                    │
│                                                    │
│                                                    │
└────────────────────────────────────────────────────┘
```

5 Things I am grateful for

1 _____
2 _____
3 _____
4 _____
5 _____

Mindfulness Exercise

(Notice five things that you can see and write them down).

# 1	
# 2	
# 3	
# 4	
# 5	

Evening Routine

This went well today

5 Things I am proud of

1 _____

2 _____

3 _____

4 _____

5 _____

This made me feel happy

My Thoughts about today

_____
_____
_____
_____
_____
_____
_____
_____
_____
_____

Morning Routine

Date: _____

Today's positive Affirmation

```
[                                                    ]
```

Today's personal Goal

(Write down what you want to achieve for yourself today)

_____

_____

Today's Intention

(Write down how you want this day to be)

```
[                                                    ]
```

5 Things I am grateful for

1 _____
2 _____
3 _____
4 _____
5 _____

Mindfulness Exercise

(Notice five things that you can see and write them down).

# 1	
# 2	
# 3	
# 4	
# 5	

Evening Routine

This went well today

5 Things I am proud of

\# 1

\# 2

\# 3

\# 4

\# 5

This made me feel happy

My Thoughts about today

Morning Routine

Date: _____

Today's positive Affirmation

```
┌─────────────────────────────────────────────────────────┐
│                                                         │
│                                                         │
│                                                         │
│                                                         │
│                                                         │
└─────────────────────────────────────────────────────────┘
```

Today's personal Goal

(Write down what you want to achieve for yourself today)

_____

_____

Today's Intention

(Write down how you want this day to be)

```
┌─────────────────────────────────────────────────────────┐
│                                                         │
│                                                         │
│                                                         │
│                                                         │
│                                                         │
└─────────────────────────────────────────────────────────┘
```

5 Things I am grateful for

1 _____
2 _____
3 _____
4 _____
5 _____

Mindfulness Exercise

(Notice five things that you can see and write them down).

# 1	
# 2	
# 3	
# 4	
# 5	

Evening Routine

This went well today

5 Things I am proud of

1

2

3

4

5

This made me feel happy

My Thoughts about today

Morning Routine

Date: _____

Today's positive Affirmation

+---+
| |
| |
| |
| |
+---+

Today's personal Goal

(Write down what you want to achieve for yourself today)

_____

_____

Today's Intention

(Write down how you want this day to be)

+---+
| |
| |
| |
| |
+---+

5 Things I am grateful for

1 _____
2 _____
3 _____
4 _____
5 _____

Mindfulness Exercise

(Notice five things that you can see and write them down).

| # 1 |
| # 2 |
| # 3 |
| # 4 |
| # 5 |

Evening Routine

This went well today

5 Things I am proud of

1 _____
2 _____
3 _____
4 _____
5 _____

This made me feel happy

My Thoughts about today

Morning Routine

Date: _____

Today's positive Affirmation

┌───┐
│   │
│   │
│   │
│   │
└───┘

Today's personal Goal

(Write down what you want to achieve for yourself today)

_____

_____

Today's Intention

(Write down how you want this day to be)

┌───┐
│   │
│   │
│   │
│   │
└───┘

5 Things I am grateful for

#1 _____

#2 _____

#3 _____

#4 _____

#5 _____

Mindfulness Exercise

(Notice five things that you can see and write them down).

#1 _____

#2 _____

#3 _____

#4 _____

#5 _____

Evening Routine

This went well today

5 Things I am proud of

1 _____

2 _____

3 _____

4 _____

5 _____

This made me feel happy

My Thoughts about today

_____
_____
_____
_____
_____
_____
_____
_____
_____

Morning Routine

Date: _____

Today's positive Affirmation

Today's personal Goal
(Write down what you want to achieve for yourself today)

Today's Intention
(Write down how you want this day to be)

5 Things I am grateful for

1
2
3
4
5

Mindfulness Exercise
(Notice five things that you can see and write them down).

# 1	
# 2	
# 3	
# 4	
# 5	

Evening Routine

This went well today

5 Things I am proud of

1 _____

2 _____

3 _____

4 _____

5 _____

This made me feel happy

My Thoughts about today

_____
_____
_____
_____
_____
_____
_____
_____
_____

Morning Routine

Date: _____

Today's positive Affirmation

| |
| |

Today's personal Goal   (Write down what you want to achieve for yourself today)

_____

_____

Today's Intention   (Write down how you want this day to be)

| |
| |

5 Things I am grateful for

1 _____
2 _____
3 _____
4 _____
5 _____

Mindfulness Exercise   (Notice five things that you can see and write them down).

| # 1 |
| # 2 |
| # 3 |
| # 4 |
| # 5 |

Evening Routine

This went well today

5 Things I am proud of

1 _____

2 _____

3 _____

4 _____

5 _____

This made me feel happy

My Thoughts about today

_____

_____

_____

_____

_____

_____

_____

_____

_____

Morning Routine

Date: _____

Today's positive Affirmation

+---+
| |
| |
| |
| |
+---+

Today's personal Goal   (Write down what you want to achieve for yourself today)

_____

_____

Today's Intention   (Write down how you want this day to be)

+---+
| |
| |
| |
| |
+---+

5 Things I am grateful for

#1 _____

#2 _____

#3 _____

#4 _____

#5 _____

Mindfulness Exercise   (Notice five things that you can see and write them down).

#1	
#2	
#3	
#4	
#5	

Evening Routine

This went well today

5 Things I am proud of

#1 _____

#2 _____

#3 _____

#4 _____

#5 _____

This made me feel happy

My Thoughts about today

_____

_____

_____

_____

_____

_____

_____

_____

_____

Morning Routine

Date: _____

Today's positive Affirmation

Today's personal Goal
(Write down what you want to achieve for yourself today)

_____

_____

Today's Intention
(Write down how you want this day to be)

5 Things I am grateful for

#1 _____
#2 _____
#3 _____
#4 _____
#5 _____

Mindfulness Exercise
(Notice five things that you can see and write them down).

#1	
#2	
#3	
#4	
#5	

Evening Routine

This went well today

5 Things I am proud of

1 _____
2 _____
3 _____
4 _____
5 _____

This made me feel happy

My Thoughts about today

_____
_____
_____
_____
_____
_____
_____
_____
_____
_____

Morning Routine

Date: _____

Today's positive Affirmation

```

```

Today's personal Goal

(Write down what you want to achieve for yourself today)

_____

_____

Today's Intention

(Write down how you want this day to be)

```

```

5 Things I am grateful for

#1 _____
#2 _____
#3 _____
#4 _____
#5 _____

Mindfulness Exercise

(Notice five things that you can see and write them down).

#1	
#2	
#3	
#4	
#5	

Evening Routine

This went well today

5 Things I am proud of

#1 _____

#2 _____

#3 _____

#4 _____

#5 _____

This made me feel happy

My Thoughts about today

_____
_____
_____
_____
_____
_____
_____
_____
_____

Morning Routine

Date: _____

Today's positive Affirmation

| |
| |

Today's personal Goal   (Write down what you want to achieve for yourself today)

_____

_____

Today's Intention   (Write down how you want this day to be)

| |
| |

5 Things I am grateful for

1 _____
2 _____
3 _____
4 _____
5 _____

Mindfulness Exercise   (Notice five things that you can see and write them down).

| # 1 |
| # 2 |
| # 3 |
| # 4 |
| # 5 |

Evening Routine

This went well today

5 Things I am proud of

#1 _____

#2 _____

#3 _____

#4 _____

#5 _____

This made me feel happy

My Thoughts about today

_____
_____
_____
_____
_____
_____
_____
_____
_____
_____
_____

Morning Routine

Date: _____

Today's positive Affirmation

```

```

Today's personal Goal

(Write down what you want to achieve for yourself today)

_____

_____

Today's Intention

(Write down how you want this day to be)

```

```

5 Things I am grateful for

#1 _____
#2 _____
#3 _____
#4 _____
#5 _____

Mindfulness Exercise

(Notice five things that you can see and write them down).

#1	
#2	
#3	
#4	
#5	

Evening Routine

This went well today

5 Things I am proud of

#1

#2

#3

#4

#5

This made me feel happy

My Thoughts about today

Morning Routine

Date: _____

Today's positive Affirmation

```
[                                                    ]
```

Today's personal Goal

(Write down what you want to achieve for yourself today)

_____

_____

Today's Intention

(Write down how you want this day to be)

```
[                                                    ]
```

5 Things I am grateful for

#1 _____
#2 _____
#3 _____
#4 _____
#5 _____

Mindfulness Exercise

(Notice five things that you can see and write them down).

#1 _____
#2 _____
#3 _____
#4 _____
#5 _____

Evening Routine

This went well today

5 Things I am proud of

1
2
3
4
5

This made me feel happy

My Thoughts about today

Morning Routine

Date: _____

Today's positive Affirmation

Today's personal Goal

(Write down what you want to achieve for yourself today)

_____

_____

Today's Intention

(Write down how you want this day to be)

5 Things I am grateful for

#1 _____

#2 _____

#3 _____

#4 _____

#5 _____

Mindfulness Exercise

(Notice five things that you can see and write them down).

| #1 |
| #2 |
| #3 |
| #4 |
| #5 |

Evening Routine

This went well today

5 Things I am proud of

1

2

3

4

5

This made me feel happy

My Thoughts about today

Morning Routine

Date: _____

Today's positive Affirmation

[ ]

Today's personal Goal

(Write down what you want to achieve for yourself today)

_____

_____

Today's Intention

(Write down how you want this day to be)

[ ]

5 Things I am grateful for

#1 _____
#2 _____
#3 _____
#4 _____
#5 _____

Mindfulness Exercise

(Notice five things that you can see and write them down).

#1 _____
#2 _____
#3 _____
#4 _____
#5 _____

Evening Routine

This went well today

5 Things I am proud of

#1
#2
#3
#4
#5

This made me feel happy

My Thoughts about today

Morning Routine

Date: _____

Today's positive Affirmation

Today's personal Goal

(Write down what you want to achieve for yourself today)

_____

_____

Today's Intention

(Write down how you want this day to be)

5 Things I am grateful for

#1 _____
#2 _____
#3 _____
#4 _____
#5 _____

Mindfulness Exercise

(Notice five things that you can see and write them down).

#1
#2
#3
#4
#5

Evening Routine

This went well today

5 Things I am proud of

#1

#2

#3

#4

#5

This made me feel happy

My Thoughts about today

Morning Routine

Date: _____

Today's positive Affirmation

Today's personal Goal   (Write down what you want to achieve for yourself today)

_____

_____

Today's Intention   (Write down how you want this day to be)

5 Things I am grateful for

#1 _____
#2 _____
#3 _____
#4 _____
#5 _____

Mindfulness Exercise   (Notice five things that you can see and write them down).

#1	
#2	
#3	
#4	
#5	

Evening Routine

This went well today

5 Things I am proud of

#1 _____

#2 _____

#3 _____

#4 _____

#5 _____

This made me feel happy

My Thoughts about today

_____
_____
_____
_____
_____
_____
_____
_____
_____
_____

Morning Routine

Date: _____

Today's positive Affirmation

```
┌─────────────────────────────────────────────────────────┐
│                                                         │
│                                                         │
│                                                         │
│                                                         │
└─────────────────────────────────────────────────────────┘
```

Today's personal Goal

(Write down what you want to achieve for yourself today)

_____

_____

Today's Intention

(Write down how you want this day to be)

```
┌─────────────────────────────────────────────────────────┐
│                                                         │
│                                                         │
│                                                         │
│                                                         │
└─────────────────────────────────────────────────────────┘
```

5 Things I am grateful for

#1 _____

#2 _____

#3 _____

#4 _____

#5 _____

Mindfulness Exercise

(Notice five things that you can see and write them down).

#1	
#2	
#3	
#4	
#5	

Evening Routine

This went well today

5 Things I am proud of

#1

#2

#3

#4

#5

This made me feel happy

My Thoughts about today

Morning Routine

Date: _____

Today's positive Affirmation

```
[                                                      ]
```

Today's personal Goal

(Write down what you want to achieve for yourself today)

_____

_____

Today's Intention

(Write down how you want this day to be)

```
[                                                      ]
```

5 Things I am grateful for

1 _____

2 _____

3 _____

4 _____

5 _____

Mindfulness Exercise

(Notice five things that you can see and write them down).

# 1	
# 2	
# 3	
# 4	
# 5	

Evening Routine

This went well today

5 Things I am proud of

\# 1 _____

\# 2 _____

\# 3 _____

\# 4 _____

\# 5 _____

This made me feel happy

My Thoughts about today

_____

_____

_____

_____

_____

_____

_____

_____

_____

_____

Morning Routine

Date: _____

Today's positive Affirmation

```
┌─────────────────────────────────────────────┐
│                                             │
│                                             │
│                                             │
│                                             │
└─────────────────────────────────────────────┘
```

Today's personal Goal

(Write down what you want to achieve for yourself today)

_____

_____

Today's Intention

(Write down how you want this day to be)

```
┌─────────────────────────────────────────────┐
│                                             │
│                                             │
│                                             │
│                                             │
└─────────────────────────────────────────────┘
```

5 Things I am grateful for

1 _____

2 _____

3 _____

4 _____

5 _____

Mindfulness Exercise

(Notice five things that you can see and write them down).

1 _____

2 _____

3 _____

4 _____

5 _____

Evening Routine

This went well today

5 Things I am proud of

#1

#2

#3

#4

#5

This made me feel happy

My Thoughts about today

Morning Routine

Date: _____

Today's positive Affirmation

Today's personal Goal

(Write down what you want to achieve for yourself today)

_____

_____

Today's Intention

(Write down how you want this day to be)

5 Things I am grateful for

#1	
#2	
#3	
#4	
#5	

Mindfulness Exercise

(Notice five things that you can see and write them down).

#1	
#2	
#3	
#4	
#5	

Evening Routine

This went well today

5 Things I am proud of

1

2

3

4

5

This made me feel happy

My Thoughts about today

Morning Routine

Date: _____

Today's positive Affirmation

```
[                                                              ]
```

Today's personal Goal

(Write down what you want to achieve for yourself today)

_____

_____

Today's Intention

(Write down how you want this day to be)

```
[                                                              ]
```

5 Things I am grateful for

#1 _____
#2 _____
#3 _____
#4 _____
#5 _____

Mindfulness Exercise

(Notice five things that you can see and write them down).

#1	
#2	
#3	
#4	
#5	

Evening Routine

This went well today

5 Things I am proud of

1

2

3

4

5

This made me feel happy

My Thoughts about today

Morning Routine

Date: _____

Today's positive Affirmation

| |
| |

Today's personal Goal

(Write down what you want to achieve for yourself today)

_____

_____

Today's Intention

(Write down how you want this day to be)

| |
| |

5 Things I am grateful for

#1 _____
#2 _____
#3 _____
#4 _____
#5 _____

Mindfulness Exercise

(Notice five things that you can see and write them down).

| #1 |
| #2 |
| #3 |
| #4 |
| #5 |

Evening Routine

This went well today

5 Things I am proud of

#1

#2

#3

#4

#5

This made me feel happy

My Thoughts about today

Morning Routine

Date: _____

Today's positive Affirmation

```
[                                                            ]
```

Today's personal Goal

(Write down what you want to achieve for yourself today)

_____
_____

Today's Intention

(Write down how you want this day to be)

```
[                                                            ]
```

5 Things I am grateful for

#1 _____
#2 _____
#3 _____
#4 _____
#5 _____

Mindfulness Exercise

(Notice five things that you can see and write them down).

#1 _____
#2 _____
#3 _____
#4 _____
#5 _____

Evening Routine

This went well today

5 Things I am proud of

1

2

3

4

5

This made me feel happy

My Thoughts about today

Morning Routine

Date: _____

Today's positive Affirmation

+---+
| |
| |
| |
+---+

Today's personal Goal

(Write down what you want to achieve for yourself today)

_____

_____

Today's Intention

(Write down how you want this day to be)

+---+
| |
| |
| |
+---+

5 Things I am grateful for

#1 _____
#2 _____
#3 _____
#4 _____
#5 _____

Mindfulness Exercise

(Notice five things that you can see and write them down).

#1	
#2	
#3	
#4	
#5	

Evening Routine

This went well today

5 Things I am proud of

#1 _____

#2 _____

#3 _____

#4 _____

#5 _____

This made me feel happy

My Thoughts about today

Morning Routine

Date: _____

Today's positive Affirmation

```
┌─────────────────────────────────────────────┐
│                                             │
│                                             │
│                                             │
│                                             │
└─────────────────────────────────────────────┘
```

Today's personal Goal   (Write down what you want to achieve for yourself today)

_____

_____

Today's Intention   (Write down how you want this day to be)

```
┌─────────────────────────────────────────────┐
│                                             │
│                                             │
│                                             │
│                                             │
└─────────────────────────────────────────────┘
```

5 Things I am grateful for

#1 _____
#2 _____
#3 _____
#4 _____
#5 _____

Mindfulness Exercise   (Notice five things that you can see and write them down).

#1	
#2	
#3	
#4	
#5	

Evening Routine

This went well today

5 Things I am proud of

#1 _____
#2 _____
#3 _____
#4 _____
#5 _____

This made me feel happy

My Thoughts about today

_____
_____
_____
_____
_____
_____
_____
_____
_____
_____

Morning Routine

Date: _____

Today's positive Affirmation

```
┌─────────────────────────────────────────┐
│                                         │
│                                         │
│                                         │
│                                         │
└─────────────────────────────────────────┘
```

Today's personal Goal

(Write down what you want to achieve for yourself today)

_____

_____

Today's Intention

(Write down how you want this day to be)

```
┌─────────────────────────────────────────┐
│                                         │
│                                         │
│                                         │
│                                         │
└─────────────────────────────────────────┘
```

5 Things I am grateful for

#1 _____

#2 _____

#3 _____

#4 _____

#5 _____

Mindfulness Exercise

(Notice five things that you can see and write them down).

#1	
#2	
#3	
#4	
#5	

Evening Routine

This went well today

5 Things I am proud of

#1

#2

#3

#4

#5

This made me feel happy

My Thoughts about today

Morning Routine

Date: _____

Today's positive Affirmation

[ ]

Today's personal Goal
(Write down what you want to achieve for yourself today)

_____
_____

Today's Intention
(Write down how you want this day to be)

[ ]

5 Things I am grateful for

#1	
#2	
#3	
#4	
#5	

Mindfulness Exercise
(Notice five things that you can see and write them down).

#1	
#2	
#3	
#4	
#5	

Evening Routine

This went well today

5 Things I am proud of

1

2

3

4

5

This made me feel happy

My Thoughts about today

Morning Routine

Date: _____

Today's positive Affirmation

| |
| |

Today's personal Goal

(Write down what you want to achieve for yourself today)

_____

_____

Today's Intention

(Write down how you want this day to be)

| |
| |

5 Things I am grateful for

# 1	
# 2	
# 3	
# 4	
# 5	

Mindfulness Exercise

(Notice five things that you can see and write them down).

# 1	
# 2	
# 3	
# 4	
# 5	

Evening Routine

This went well today

5 Things I am proud of

#1
#2
#3
#4
#5

This made me feel happy

My Thoughts about today

Morning Routine

Date: _____

Today's positive Affirmation

```
[                                                              ]
```

Today's personal Goal

(Write down what you want to achieve for yourself today)

_____

_____

Today's Intention

(Write down how you want this day to be)

```
[                                                              ]
```

5 Things I am grateful for

#1 _____

#2 _____

#3 _____

#4 _____

#5 _____

Mindfulness Exercise

(Notice five things that you can see and write them down).

| #1 |
| #2 |
| #3 |
| #4 |
| #5 |

Evening Routine

This went well today

5 Things I am proud of

#1 _____

#2 _____

#3 _____

#4 _____

#5 _____

This made me feel happy

My Thoughts about today

_____
_____
_____
_____
_____
_____
_____
_____
_____

Morning Routine

Date: _____

Today's positive Affirmation

[   ]

Today's personal Goal

(Write down what you want to achieve for yourself today)

_____

_____

Today's Intention

(Write down how you want this day to be)

[   ]

5 Things I am grateful for

#1 _____
#2 _____
#3 _____
#4 _____
#5 _____

Mindfulness Exercise

(Notice five things that you can see and write them down).

#1	
#2	
#3	
#4	
#5	

Evening Routine

This went well today

5 Things I am proud of

1 _____

2 _____

3 _____

4 _____

5 _____

This made me feel happy

My Thoughts about today

_____
_____
_____
_____
_____
_____
_____
_____
_____

Morning Routine

Date: _____

Today's positive Affirmation

```
┌─────────────────────────────────────────────────────────────┐
│                                                             │
│                                                             │
│                                                             │
│                                                             │
└─────────────────────────────────────────────────────────────┘
```

Today's personal Goal

(Write down what you want to achieve for yourself today)

_____

_____

Today's Intention

(Write down how you want this day to be)

```
┌─────────────────────────────────────────────────────────────┐
│                                                             │
│                                                             │
│                                                             │
│                                                             │
└─────────────────────────────────────────────────────────────┘
```

5 Things I am grateful for

1 _____

2 _____

3 _____

4 _____

5 _____

Mindfulness Exercise

(Notice five things that you can see and write them down).

# 1	
# 2	
# 3	
# 4	
# 5	

Evening Routine

This went well today

5 Things I am proud of

#1

#2

#3

#4

#5

This made me feel happy

My Thoughts about today

Morning Routine

Date: _____

Today's positive Affirmation

```


```

Today's personal Goal

(Write down what you want to achieve for yourself today)

_____

_____

Today's Intention

(Write down how you want this day to be)

```


```

5 Things I am grateful for

#1	
#2	
#3	
#4	
#5	

Mindfulness Exercise

(Notice five things that you can see and write them down).

#1	
#2	
#3	
#4	
#5	

Evening Routine

This went well today

5 Things I am proud of

#1

#2

#3

#4

#5

This made me feel happy

My Thoughts about today

Morning Routine

Date: _____

Today's positive Affirmation

```



```

Today's personal Goal

(Write down what you want to achieve for yourself today)

_____

_____

Today's Intention

(Write down how you want this day to be)

```



```

5 Things I am grateful for

#1 _____
#2 _____
#3 _____
#4 _____
#5 _____

Mindfulness Exercise

(Notice five things that you can see and write them down).

#1	
#2	
#3	
#4	
#5	

Evening Routine

This went well today

5 Things I am proud of

#1

#2

#3

#4

#5

This made me feel happy

My Thoughts about today

Morning Routine

Date: _____

Today's positive Affirmation

Today's personal Goal

(Write down what you want to achieve for yourself today)

_____

_____

Today's Intention

(Write down how you want this day to be)

5 Things I am grateful for

#1	
#2	
#3	
#4	
#5	

Mindfulness Exercise

(Notice five things that you can see and write them down).

#1	
#2	
#3	
#4	
#5	

Evening Routine

This went well today

5 Things I am proud of

#1

#2

#3

#4

#5

This made me feel happy

My Thoughts about today

Morning Routine

Date: _____

Today's positive Affirmation

```
[                                                    ]
```

Today's personal Goal
(Write down what you want to achieve for yourself today)

_____

_____

Today's Intention
(Write down how you want this day to be)

```
[                                                    ]
```

5 Things I am grateful for

#1 _____
#2 _____
#3 _____
#4 _____
#5 _____

Mindfulness Exercise
(Notice five things that you can see and write them down).

#1 _____
#2 _____
#3 _____
#4 _____
#5 _____

Evening Routine

This went well today

5 Things I am proud of

#1

#2

#3

#4

#5

This made me feel happy

My Thoughts about today

Morning Routine

Date: _____

Today's positive Affirmation

```
[                                                      ]
```

Today's personal Goal

(Write down what you want to achieve for yourself today)

_____

_____

Today's Intention

(Write down how you want this day to be)

```
[                                                      ]
```

5 Things I am grateful for

# 1	
# 2	
# 3	
# 4	
# 5	

Mindfulness Exercise

(Notice five things that you can see and write them down).

# 1	
# 2	
# 3	
# 4	
# 5	

Evening Routine

This went well today

5 Things I am proud of

1

2

3

4

5

This made me feel happy

My Thoughts about today

Morning Routine

Date: _____

Today's positive Affirmation

```
[                                                              ]
```

Today's personal Goal

(Write down what you want to achieve for yourself today)

_____

_____

Today's Intention

(Write down how you want this day to be)

```
[                                                              ]
```

5 Things I am grateful for

#1 _____
#2 _____
#3 _____
#4 _____
#5 _____

Mindfulness Exercise

(Notice five things that you can see and write them down).

#1	
#2	
#3	
#4	
#5	

Evening Routine

This went well today

5 Things I am proud of

#1 _____

#2 _____

#3 _____

#4 _____

#5 _____

This made me feel happy

My Thoughts about today

_____
_____
_____
_____
_____
_____
_____
_____
_____

Morning Routine

Date: _____

Today's positive Affirmation

```
[                                                        ]
```

Today's personal Goal

(Write down what you want to achieve for yourself today)

_____

_____

Today's Intention

(Write down how you want this day to be)

```
[                                                        ]
```

5 Things I am grateful for

1 _____
2 _____
3 _____
4 _____
5 _____

Mindfulness Exercise

(Notice five things that you can see and write them down).

# 1	
# 2	
# 3	
# 4	
# 5	

Evening Routine

This went well today

5 Things I am proud of

1

2

3

4

5

This made me feel happy

My Thoughts about today

Morning Routine

Date: _____

Today's positive Affirmation

```


```

Today's personal Goal   (Write down what you want to achieve for yourself today)

_____

_____

Today's Intention   (Write down how you want this day to be)

```


```

5 Things I am grateful for

#1 _____
#2 _____
#3 _____
#4 _____
#5 _____

Mindfulness Exercise   (Notice five things that you can see and write them down).

#1
#2
#3
#4
#5

Evening Routine

This went well today

5 Things I am proud of

1

2

3

4

5

This made me feel happy

My Thoughts about today

Morning Routine

Date: _____

Today's positive Affirmation

_____
| |
| |
| |
| |
|_____|

Today's personal Goal

(Write down what you want to achieve for yourself today)

_____

_____

Today's Intention

(Write down how you want this day to be)

_____
| |
| |
| |
| |
|_____|

5 Things I am grateful for

1 _____

2 _____

3 _____

4 _____

5 _____

Mindfulness Exercise

(Notice five things that you can see and write them down).

# 1	
# 2	
# 3	
# 4	
# 5	

Evening Routine

This went well today

5 Things I am proud of

1 _____

2 _____

3 _____

4 _____

5 _____

This made me feel happy

My Thoughts about today

_____
_____
_____
_____
_____
_____
_____
_____
_____
_____

Morning Routine

Date: _____

Today's positive Affirmation

_____

Today's personal Goal   (Write down what you want to achieve for yourself today)

_____

_____

Today's Intention   (Write down how you want this day to be)

_____

5 Things I am grateful for

#1 _____
#2 _____
#3 _____
#4 _____
#5 _____

Mindfulness Exercise   (Notice five things that you can see and write them down).

#1 _____
#2 _____
#3 _____
#4 _____
#5 _____

Evening Routine

This went well today

5 Things I am proud of

1 _____

2 _____

3 _____

4 _____

5 _____

This made me feel happy

My Thoughts about today

_____

_____

_____

_____

_____

_____

_____

_____

_____

_____

Morning Routine

Date: _____

Today's positive Affirmation

Today's personal Goal

(Write down what you want to achieve for yourself today)

_____

_____

Today's Intention

(Write down how you want this day to be)

5 Things I am grateful for

#1 _____
#2 _____
#3 _____
#4 _____
#5 _____

Mindfulness Exercise

(Notice five things that you can see and write them down).

#1
#2
#3
#4
#5

Evening Routine

This went well today

5 Things I am proud of

#1

#2

#3

#4

#5

This made me feel happy

My Thoughts about today

Morning Routine

Date: _____

Today's positive Affirmation

```

```

Today's personal Goal   (Write down what you want to achieve for yourself today)

_____

_____

Today's Intention   (Write down how you want this day to be)

```

```

5 Things I am grateful for

1 _____
2 _____
3 _____
4 _____
5 _____

Mindfulness Exercise   (Notice five things that you can see and write them down).

# 1	
# 2	
# 3	
# 4	
# 5	

Evening Routine

This went well today

5 Things I am proud of

#1 _____

#2 _____

#3 _____

#4 _____

#5 _____

This made me feel happy

My Thoughts about today

_____

_____

_____

_____

_____

_____

_____

_____

_____

Morning Routine

Date: _____

Today's positive Affirmation

> (blank box)

Today's personal Goal

(Write down what you want to achieve for yourself today)

_____
_____

Today's Intention

(Write down how you want this day to be)

> (blank box)

5 Things I am grateful for

1 _____
2 _____
3 _____
4 _____
5 _____

Mindfulness Exercise

(Notice five things that you can see and write them down).

# 1	
# 2	
# 3	
# 4	
# 5	

Evening Routine

This went well today

5 Things I am proud of

#1
#2
#3
#4
#5

This made me feel happy

My Thoughts about today

Morning Routine

Date: _____

Today's positive Affirmation

Today's personal Goal
(Write down what you want to achieve for yourself today)

Today's Intention
(Write down how you want this day to be)

5 Things I am grateful for

#1 _____
#2 _____
#3 _____
#4 _____
#5 _____

Mindfulness Exercise
(Notice five things that you can see and write them down).

#1	
#2	
#3	
#4	
#5	

Evening Routine

This went well today

5 Things I am proud of

#1

#2

#3

#4

#5

This made me feel happy

My Thoughts about today

Morning Routine

Date: _____

Today's positive Affirmation

```



```

Today's personal Goal (Write down what you want to achieve for yourself today)

_____

_____

Today's Intention (Write down how you want this day to be)

```



```

5 Things I am grateful for

#1	
#2	
#3	
#4	
#5	

Mindfulness Exercise (Notice five things that you can see and write them down).

#1	
#2	
#3	
#4	
#5	

Evening Routine

This went well today

5 Things I am proud of

#1

#2

#3

#4

#5

This made me feel happy

My Thoughts about today

Morning Routine

Date: _____

Today's positive Affirmation

Today's personal Goal

(Write down what you want to achieve for yourself today)

_____

_____

Today's Intention

(Write down how you want this day to be)

5 Things I am grateful for

#1 _____

#2 _____

#3 _____

#4 _____

#5 _____

Mindfulness Exercise

(Notice five things that you can see and write them down).

#1 _____

#2 _____

#3 _____

#4 _____

#5 _____

Evening Routine

This went well today

5 Things I am proud of

1

2

3

4

5

This made me feel happy

My Thoughts about today

Morning Routine

Date: _____

Today's positive Affirmation

```
┌─────────────────────────────────────────────────────┐
│                                                     │
│                                                     │
│                                                     │
│                                                     │
└─────────────────────────────────────────────────────┘
```

Today's personal Goal

(Write down what you want to achieve for yourself today)

_____

_____

Today's Intention

(Write down how you want this day to be)

```
┌─────────────────────────────────────────────────────┐
│                                                     │
│                                                     │
│                                                     │
│                                                     │
└─────────────────────────────────────────────────────┘
```

5 Things I am grateful for

1
2
3
4
5

Mindfulness Exercise

(Notice five things that you can see and write them down).

1
2
3
4
5

Evening Routine

This went well today

5 Things I am proud of

#1

#2

#3

#4

#5

This made me feel happy

My Thoughts about today

Morning Routine

Date: _____

Today's positive Affirmation

```
[                                                            ]
```

Today's personal Goal

(Write down what you want to achieve for yourself today)

_____

_____

Today's Intention

(Write down how you want this day to be)

```
[                                                            ]
```

5 Things I am grateful for

1 _____
2 _____
3 _____
4 _____
5 _____

Mindfulness Exercise

(Notice five things that you can see and write them down).

# 1	
# 2	
# 3	
# 4	
# 5	

Evening Routine

This went well today

5 Things I am proud of

#1

#2

#3

#4

#5

This made me feel happy

My Thoughts about today

Printed in Great Britain
by Amazon